How to
Read and Write
Poems

by Margaret Ryan

FRANKLIN WATTS
NEW YORK/LONDON/TORONTO/SYDNEY
1991
A FIRST BOOK

Cover photograph copyright © Karen Quigley

Photographs copyright ©: Pictorial Parade Inc.: pp. 7, 16 (Lambert Studios);
Unicorn Stock Photos: pp. 8 (Floren Thompson), 55 (A. Gurmankin);
FPG International: pp. 17 (C. Smith), 38 (E. Nagele), 47 (Ralph Cowan);
Comstock, Inc.: 18, 25 (Bonnie Kamin), 35, 50 (both R. Michael Stuckey);
Art Resource, Inc., N.Y.: pp. 20, 52 bottom (both Scala), 41 (Giraudon);
The Bettmann Archive: pp. 22, 52 top; The Pierpont Morgan Library, N.Y.,
(MA214): p. 30; Poets in Public Service: p. 59.

Library of Congress Cataloging-in-Publication Data

Ryan, Margaret.
How to read and write poems / by Margaret Ryan.
p.   cm.—(A First book)
Includes bibliographical references and index.
Summary: Introduces the basic poetic concepts of rhythm, meter,
imagery, and rhyme and demonstrates how to write different kinds of
poems from haiku to limerick.
ISBN 0-531-20043-4
1. Poetics—Juvenile literature. [1. Poetry. 2. Creative
writing.] I. Title. II. Series.
PN1042.R88   1991
808.1—dc20   91-12141   CIP   AC

CONTENTS

CHAPTER ONE

WHAT IS A POEM?

Poetry is a very old art form, older than novels, short stories, and plays. Poetry is probably even older than written language. The first poets may have memorized their verses and recited them aloud long before the invention of the alphabet, paper, or pens.

But while poetry has been around almost forever, even the experts can't agree on a single, simple definition.

What the Poets Say

Many poets have tried to define poetry. Some link it with truth. Louis MacNeice, an Irish poet, said poetry must be honest even before it is beautiful. And Samuel Johnson called poetry "the art of uniting pleasure with truth."

Other poets define poetry by comparing it with prose, the language of novels and newspapers. Samuel Taylor Coleridge contrasted the two this way: "Prose—words in their best order; poetry—the best words in their best order."

Edgar Allan Poe called poetry "the rhythmical creation of beauty" in words. "Poetry is a way of taking life by the throat," Robert Frost wrote, and Carl Sandburg defined it as "the synthesis of hyacinths and biscuits," a combination of the beautiful and the useful.

"Poetry is all nouns and verbs," according to Marianne Moore. And poetry *is* made up of words. But not all nouns and verbs add up to poetry. In her poem called "Poetry," Moore offered another definition, saying that poets can present for inspection "imaginary gardens with real toads in them."

Imagination

Poetry does combine the real and the imaginary, sometimes with startling effects. Emily Dickinson defined poetry by the way it made her feel: "If I read a book and it makes my whole body so cold no fire ever can warm me, I know that is poetry. If I feel physically as if the top of my head were taken off, I know that is poetry. These are the only ways I know it."

The modern American poets
Robert Frost (above left),
Carl Sandburg (above right),
and Marianne Moore (left)
all had original ideas
about poetry.

Poetry may not make your hair stand on end, or give you chills, but it can affect you physically, too, making your heart beat faster or bringing tears to your eyes.

Poetry has this power because it acts on the imagination. And what you imagine fully, you experience as real. If you've ever pictured yourself biting into a lemon and felt saliva flood your mouth in response to the imagined bitterness, you have some idea of the imagination's power. Poetry runs on that power the way cars run on gasoline. Through

With poetry we share private experience. "Autobiographia Literaria," by Frank O'Hara, is about how the poet reaches outward from within.

the imagination, poetry transmits the poet's feelings, immediately, to you. You catch the poet's feeling, the way you might catch someone else's cold. Consider this example:

AUTOBIOGRAPHIA LITERARIA

When I was a child
I played by myself in a
corner of the schoolyard
all alone.

I hated dolls and I
hated games, animals were
not friendly and birds
flew away.

If anyone was looking
for me I hid behind a
tree and cried out "I am
an orphan."

And here I am, the
center of all beauty!
writing these poems!
Imagine!
   —Frank O'Hara

The title of the poem means "literary autobiography," the story of a writer's own life. Did you see the child alone in the schoolyard in your mind's eye as you read? Did you hear a voice cry out in your imagination? Could you picture the birds flying away? Did you feel the child's loneliness and sense how it changed to excitement by the poem's end?

If you can answer yes to any of these questions, you "caught" the poet's feelings. You experienced some of poetry's power.

The Question of Rhyme

Some people say it's easy to recognize poetry: poetry is anything that rhymes. Yet not all poems rhyme, as Frank O'Hara's picture of his childhood shows.

The fact is, verse has to rhyme; poetry doesn't. What's the difference?

We use verse—lines that have a regular beat and a pattern of rhymes—for other things besides poetry: messages in birthday cards, jump rope rhymes, ways to remember facts (like "*i* before *e*, except after *c*"), and advertising jingles. Verses can be fun, playful, even useful. But they are not always poetry, because they don't always express and share something true and mysterious about the writer's life.

On the other hand, many wonderful poems are not written in verse. Some poems have no regular pattern of rhythm or rhyme. Instead, these poems use language that is natural yet charged with feeling, the kinds of words and rhythms you use when you talk to close friends about how you feel.

Sometimes rhyme is fashionable, and sometimes it's not. Rhyme can enhance a poem and our pleasure in a poem. But rhyme is not essential to poetry.

No Formulas

Unlike math or science, poetry can't be reduced to formulas. But poetry can be precise about things—like wishes and dreams—that might otherwise remain cloudy. And poetry's power lets us discover and communicate truths about ourselves and the world.

So it isn't easy to say what poetry is. But we can say what it does: poetry lets us share experience—the private world of thoughts, desires, memories, sensations, and dreams—through our imagination. That experience is communicated, of course, through words.

CHAPTER TWO

HOW TO READ A POEM

In a famous poem about the art of poetry, Archibald MacLeish wrote, "A poem should not mean/But be."

True, a poem doesn't have to mean. Like a door or a window, a poem just is. You don't have to understand people fully in order to like them and to enjoy them. You can like a poem without understanding it, or all of it, too. You can like the words it uses, the pictures it creates in your mind as you read or hear it, the music of it. You can like it because it reminds you of something that happened to you.

Yet many people wonder what poems mean and how they mean it.

Begin at the Beginning

Titles can tell what a poem is about, who is speaking, or what form the poem is written in.

A poem called "The Nightingale," for example, will probably be about a bird that sings. "The River Merchant to His Wife: A Letter" will be just that. A dirge is a sad song. A sonnet is a poem with fourteen lines, each ten syllables long, rhymed in a particular pattern. A sestina, like a sonnet, has a predictable form. So does a haiku, a limerick, and a villanelle.

Next, consider how the poem looks. Is it long and skinny, short and fat? Is it made up of stanzas—groups of lines—of equal length? Or is the poem in the shape of something else—a bottle, or a pair of wings? Think about the shape of the poem as you read.

What Do the Words Say?

Now read the poem through. Better yet, read it aloud. You can get someone else to read it to you, or you can listen to a recording of the poet or an actor reading it.

Think about the meaning of the words. What are the facts of the poem? What is it about? Can you describe the character of the person speaking through the poem? Who is that speaker talking to? Where are they as they speak? How do they feel? What's the main message you receive?

Digging Deeper

If you don't know what some of the words in the poem mean, look them up.

Some words have more than one meaning. Does *curious* mean "nosy" or does it mean "odd"? Does *hearth* mean the floor of a fireplace, or the home and family life?

You don't always have to choose. Like two notes that form a chord, the combination of different meanings can add depth and richness to a poem.

Finding Comparisons

We use language in different ways and for different reasons. Sometimes, we just want to state the facts. Other times, we try to create a forceful or dramatic impression.

For example, if you got lost on the way to a friend's house, you might arrive at last and say, "I took the wrong road." You would be using language literally, to state a fact.

But if you showed up at your twentieth high school reunion, and someone asked how you became a gangster, you might also say, "I took the wrong road." In this case, you would be using language figuratively. You would be comparing your life to a journey, saying your choices were like roads and that you had made a choice that caused you to become "lost."

Because poets explore the nature of language and the human condition, and try to communicate strongly and dramatically to the imaginations of their readers, poems often use language figuratively.

Poets aren't the only ones who use language this way. You probably use one figure of speech, comparison, all the time. You might describe someone as funny as a monkey, playful as a kitten, silly as a goose. "He's a real tiger," we say about someone fierce. Or "I was quiet as a mouse."

Since poetry often communicates what is private and mysterious and unknowable, comparison is a valuable tool. In fact, it is one of poetry's chief ways of communicating.

Similes

Some comparisons tell you what's being compared very clearly. They use the word *like* or *as*—blind as a bat, for example, or built like a Mack truck—and are called similes.

Poets use similes to express the nature of the people they love:

My love is like a red, red rose . . . [Robert Burns]

Does Robert Burns's famous simile help you to capture what he was feeling?

You are like the spring earth, my love . . . [Nazim Hikmet]
Similes can tell how the world looks and feels:

Think of the storm roaming the sky uneasily like a dog looking for a place to sleep in, listen to it growling . . . [Elizabeth Bishop]

16

The folk song "Sometimes I feel like a motherless child" uses similes to communicate feelings. The song begins "Sometimes I feel like a motherless child" and then compares the singer's feelings to other things:

Sometimes I feel like I have no friend . . .

Sometimes I feel like I never been born . . .

Sometimes I feel like a feather in air . . .

Sometimes I feel like I'm almost gone . . .

"Sometimes I feel like a motherless child . . . a long, long way from home."

What do you think the main feeling of the song is, happy or sad? What if the song said, "Sometimes I feel lonely" instead of "Sometimes I feel like a motherless child"? Which is easier to see in the mind's eye?

Most people can picture a motherless child easily but have trouble seeing "lonely." We say "motherless child" is concrete and specific. Because it does not appeal to the senses, we say "lonely" is abstract.

"Motherless child" is also more complicated than "lonely." A motherless child might feel frightened, abandoned, vulnerable, scared, sad, *and* lonely.

Metaphor

Sometimes poets compare one thing to another without saying "like" or "as." They write "This *is* that" when they mean "This is *like* that."

For example, Denise Levertov wrote, "Goodness was a fever in you." She means "Goodness was like a fever in you."

Comparisons that don't use *like* or *as* are called metaphors. Metaphors are a mild form of magic,

Italian painter Giuseppe Arcimboldo (ca. 1527–1593)
played with visual metaphors. Look at this gentleman.
His nose is a red pepper; his cheeks, peaches;
his fingers, white radishes.

making it possible to turn abstractions—like goodness, innocence, sorrow, joy, love, or hate—into things you can see, hear, taste, touch, or smell.

Metaphors aren't just for poets. We say, "Life is just a bowl of cherries" when things are going well, or "You are my sunshine" to someone who brightens our days. One class of fourth-graders described the school day this way: "Time is a turtle. It moves too slow."

Because there's no "like" or "as" to tip you off, metaphors can be harder to spot than similes. See if you can find the metaphors in the following poem.

MISS BLUES'ES CHILD

If the blues would let me,
Lord knows I would smile.
If the blues would let me,
I would smile, smile, smile.
Instead of that I'm cryin'—
I must be Miss Blues'es child.

You were my moon up in the sky,
At night my wishing star.
I love you, oh, I love you so—
But you have gone so far!

Now my days are lonely,
And night-time drives me wild.
In my heart I'm crying,
I'm just Miss Blues'es child.
                    —Langston Hughes

The whole poem is built on a metaphor: the poet is so sad he is like a child of the blues. The blues is like a person: Miss Blues.

21

Langston Hughes (1902–1967), American poet

"You were my moon up in the sky" is a metaphor, too. It means "You were like the moon up in the sky to me." The line gives us a sense of the loved one's distance, mystery, and power.

Repetition

Did you notice the repetition in "Miss Blues'es Child"? The third and fourth lines repeat the first two lines, with a small variation. The word *smile* is repeated three times after it first appears. "I love you" is repeated in the ninth line. And the long *i* sound is repeated often, in the rhymes *smile, child,* and *wild,* as well as in words like *drive* and *cryin'.*

If you didn't notice the repetitions much, that's probably because you expected them. Almost every poem involves repetition of something, somewhere.

In the days before written language, repetition made poems easier to memorize and repeat. Repetition is also an important part of human life. Day follows night in a predictable pattern; the seasons follow each other in order each year.

Repetition creates patterns, which give shape and order to our lives. In life and in poetry, variation keeps repetition interesting, as changing weather keeps every day from being exactly like another.

Notice how Langston Hughes varied the line he repeated: "Lord knows I would smile" became "I would smile, smile, smile" the second time around.

Rhythm

Rhythm is a kind of repetition, too. The word *rhythm* comes from a Greek word meaning recurring motion. The rhythm of poetry is similar to the beat in music.

Like repetition, rhythm is a fact of life. Our hearts beat in a rhythm as the muscle expands and contracts, pumping blood through the body. Our bodies have other rhythms, too: the pattern of our breathing, the rhythm of the way we walk or run.

The best way to learn about rhythm is by listening: to the beat of your heart, the pattern of your steps, the flow of your breath, the world you live in.

Poets use the rhythms of language to communicate what the world feels like. Lines can gallop or saunter or stall if a poet is good with rhythm. Notice the different rhythms of the following lines:

Busy old fool, unruly Sun . . . [John Donne]

Shall I compare thee to a summer's day?
[William Shakespeare]

Repetition can be pleasing.
Rhythm in poetry is a form of repetition.

Alligator pie, alligator pie,
If I don't get some I think I'm gonna die . . .
[Dennis Lee]
The first line sounds busy; the second line is more leisurely; the last two lines seem to bounce.

Feet

Poets measure rhythm in units called feet. In English, a foot can be two or three syllables long. The most common foot is called the iamb. An iambic foot has two syllables, with the accent on the second one. The word *above* is an example of an iamb. Although lines may be written mostly in one meter, there is often variation within a single line. Other rhythmic units in English are:

· the trochee—two syllables, accent on the first: "headache"
   By the shores of Gitche Gumee . . . [Henry Wadsworth Longfellow]
· the dactyl—three syllables, accent on the first: "terrible"
   In Brueghel's great picture, The Kermess . . . [William Carlos Williams]

· the anapest—three syllables, accent on the last: "halloween"

And the widows of Ashur are loud in their wail . . . [Lord Byron]

· the spondee—two syllables, both stressed: "head-first"

(Whole lines are rarely written in spondees.)

Poets measure lines of poetry by how many feet there are in a line. Lines with five iambic feet are said to be written in iambic pentameter. Here is a line written in iambic pentameter:

The woods decay, the woods decay and fall . . .

Feet are handy ways to measure, but they are somewhat artificial.

Many contemporary poets ignore measured lines and write as people talk, with a little more shape. Here is the beginning of a poem that relies more on speech than on feet for its rhythm:

HORSES

I look across some ragged meadows
where I played in summers years before.
Over the neighbor's fence, three horses—
two chestnuts and a dappled gray.

They have been free all night
without a scrap of leather on them,
grazing, huddling close, or moving lazily about.
They seem to have the world to themselves. . . .
　　　　　　　—Robert Winner

Rhyme

Rhyme is another form of repetition—the repetition of similar sounds.

　　Used at the ends of lines, rhymes help give poems shape. The pattern in which rhyme words appear is called a rhyme scheme. We use letters to represent each rhyme sound. Here is an example of a rhyme scheme:

ANDRE

I had a dream last night. I dreamed　[a]
I had to pick a mother out.　[b]
I had to choose a father too.　[c]
At first, I wondered what to do,　[c]
There were so many there, it seemed,　[a]
Short and tall and thin and stout.　[b]

But just before I sprang awake.　[d]
I knew what parents I would take.　[d]

And this surprised and made me glad:　[e]
They were the ones I always had!　[e]
　　　　　　　—Gwendolyn Brooks

28

Rhyme can do more than stitch a stanza together. Words that sound alike invite us to think
about what else they have in common. In "Miss
Blues'es Child," (see page 21) "smile" rhymes with
"child" in the first stanza; in the third stanza, it
rhymes with "wild." In the middle stanza, "star"
rhymes with "far." A child might be happy and
smiling, but this one is wild. A star is beautiful and
desirable; it is also distant.

If there are rhymes in the poem you want to
understand, think about what they add to the poem's
meaning.

Putting It All Together

Once you have looked at all of the different ele-
ments of a poem, read the poem again. Has your
understanding of the poem been enriched? Do you
appreciate the poet's craft more? When all of the
parts of a poem work together, the poem is like a
powerful engine, built of words, that carries the
poet's feelings to you.

Is It Good?

Sometimes you will be asked to judge a poem, to
say if it is good or not.

To Mariane Reynolds —

Much have I travell'd in the Realms of gold
    And many goodly States and Kingdoms seen
    Round many western islands have I been
Which Bards in fealty to Apollo hold
Oft of one wide expanse had I been told
    That deep brow'd Homer ruled as his Demesne
    Yet could I never judge what Men could mean
Till I heard Chapman speak out loud and bold
    Then felt I like some Watcher of the Skies
    When a new Planet swims into his Ken
Or like stout Cortez when with eagle eyes
    He star'd at the Pacific and all his Men
Look at each other with a wild surmise
    Silent upon a Peak in Darien —

Original manuscript of the sonnet
"On First Looking into Chapman's Homer,"
by John Keats. It begins, "Much have I
travell'd in the realms of gold."

This is a difficult task. Poems are like food; everyone has different "taste buds," different experiences, different reasons for liking what they like. Styles change, and tastes change, too. A poem considered good today might seem silly in a dozen years or more.

Just because a poem is in a book or printed in a magazine doesn't mean it's good. The fact that a poem is typewritten or handwritten doesn't affect its value, either.

It's important to know what you like about poems, what makes them good for you. Try copying poems you enjoy into a notebook. As you read through your collection, you will begin to understand what you admire.

CHAPTER THREE

HOW TO WRITE A POEM

Sometimes poems are easy to write. The words that express how you feel arrive as if by magic in your head and make their way without effort onto paper. When you look at them again, they sing.

But sometimes it is hard to write poems. In fact, it can be hard to write anything well, even for people who are very talented.

W. B. Yeats, one of the greatest poets of our century, wrote about how hard he found writing poetry: "Nothing is done upon the first day, not one rhyme is in place; and when at last the rhymes begin to come, the first rough draft of a six line stanza takes the whole day."

Don't let this discourage you. It's hard work to be excellent at anything. To be a professional tennis player takes total commitment, but many people learn to play well enough to enjoy an occasional game. Without too much effort, it's possible to write poetry the way you play tennis or dance or paint—just for the fun of it.

You don't need much equipment to write poetry. You probably have it all: the spark of creativity and originality that comes with being human; the language you use every day and your own voice; your dreams, wishes, feelings, memories, hopes, doubts, and fears; a piece of paper; and a pencil or a pen.

Find a place to write where you can be alone with your thoughts. If you can manage the inner quiet that lets you hear the words of poetry as they arise inside you, your work will be easier.

Getting Started

Ideas for poems come from many places. Some poets write to answer other poems or because of something that happened to them long ago, or just today. Other poets write for revenge or to get attention.

The important thing is to write about things you feel strongly about. Many students like to write about their pets, their friends, their brothers, sisters, parents, or grandparents. Others like to write about special places they've visited.

But don't limit yourself when you think about

what to write. Lots of things you might not consider poetic can appear in poems: lug nuts and whitewall tires and bicycles and factories and the stock market.

Follow the advice of the poet Rilke when searching for subject matter. He advised a young poet to get close to nature, to say "what you see and experience and love and lose."

Try to stay away from general themes like love and death. Instead, write about everyday life, using the things around you, the images from your dreams, and things you remember vividly to express yourself.

Appeal to the Senses

When you write a poem, include things you can see, hear, touch, taste, and smell. This will make it easier for your reader to catch what you want to share.

For instance, say you are writing about a trip to the beach. Some students might write about it this way:

I spent the day at the beach.
It was hot.
I was happy.
We bought ice cream and ate it.
I went into the ocean with my dad.

34

One way to start writing poetry is to
think about what you have seen, heard,
smelled, tasted, felt. Summon the sensations
of a day at the beach, for example.

But see how much easier it is to enter into the day at the beach when you include detail that appeals to the senses.

Waves crashed on the sand.
Turquoise and white and orange
beach umbrellas dotted the shore.
I found a broken conch shell, a perfect scallop.
The sand was gritty and hot underfoot.
Ice cream was smooth and cold on my tongue.
I could smell seaweed and suntan oil.
When the wave washed over me,
I held onto my dad's hand.

Concrete, Specific

Many poets have trouble being concrete and specific. They write, "It's nice to be happy" instead of telling what being happy really feels like ("Sometimes I feel like a big brass band") or what things—Oreo cookies, hot chocolate, football games, autumn leaves cracking underfoot, a white kitten named Polo—make them happy.

If you need practice in being concrete, try this.

Begin each line of your poem with "Sometimes I feel like . . ." Then list something that conveys your mood.

Sometimes I feel like a volcano.
Sometimes I feel like a Lamborghini.
Sometimes I feel like a red rose.

Next, add an action:
Sometimes I feel like a volcano
   spilling hot lava into the sea.
Sometimes I feel like a Lamborghini speeding
   along a winding country road.
Sometimes I feel like a red rose
   opening its petals in the sun.
Once you've gotten started, see where your imagination takes you.

Writing Metaphors

You can also write a series of metaphors that appeal to the senses. Notice how this poem turns the moon into something you can see, hear, taste, smell, and touch.

THE MOON

   is an orchestra playing
   a white waterlily
      in the dark pond of the sky

What does the moon look like to you?

a flashlight
a scoop of vanilla ice cream
the bald head of the sun's cold husband.
　　　—Class poem, seventh grade,
　　　　　Pelham Junior High

Try it yourself. Pick an object you can see from where you are sitting right now, something that has some meaning or mystery for you. Then write metaphors that appeal to the senses.

Let's say you choose the maple tree you can see from your bedroom window. Look at the tree (or whatever you chose) and see what you can turn it into. What does it look like? An old woman with her arms raised? Good. Write that down.

　　　The maple tree is an old woman
　　　　with her arms raised.

Now, what does the tree sound like? If it isn't making any noise, think about what it would sound like if it did—a banshee howling? A pack of dogs scratching to get out?

What would it taste like? Maple syrup? A fat mint toothpick?

What would it feel like? Smell like?

Build a whole poem of your metaphors, following your ideas wherever they lead.

Writing a Haiku

Another way to write a poem is to begin with a form, such as the haiku. The form of the haiku is easy to remember: just three lines, with the first and last line shorter than the middle line.

Some people think that the haiku should have seventeen syllables, five in the first line, seven in the second, five in the third. You don't have to be that strict.

Like many other forms of poetry, haiku form is linked to a particular content. Haiku tend to be about everyday occurrences and to include images from nature. They are moments of intense noticing, a snapshot of something you see, hear, feel, taste, or smell. Here are some examples.

> *Will it soon be spring?*
> *They lay the ground-work for us,*
> *the plum tree and the moon.*
> —Basho

> *With what voice*
> *and what song would you sing, spider,*
> *in this autumn breeze?*
> —Basho

A haiku is a
short poem that
freezes a moment in time.

ALBA

As cool as the pale wet leaves
Of lily-of-the-valley
She lay beside me in the dawn.
      —Ezra Pound

Try writing a haiku. You could write one about each season or one for each month. Or write a series of haiku about your favorite holidays.

Writing a Limerick

Another form you might enjoy is called the limerick. Try to figure out the limerick's form from this example:

There was an old man of Blackheath
Who sat on his set of false teeth
Said he, with a start,
"O Lord, bless my heart!
I have bitten myself underneath!"
      —Anonymous

Limericks are five lines long. Their rhythm is based on the anapest: a strong accent followed by two weak ones. Lines 1, 2, and 5 each have three beats, and all rhyme with each other. Lines 3 and 4 have two beats and rhyme with each other.

Limericks tend to be silly; in fact, many of them are sheer nonsense, built of wit and wordplay. Sometimes limericks are even naughty. See if you can write a limerick or two. Can you write a serious limerick? Give it a try!

CHAPTER FOUR

REVISING POEMS

When you've finished a writing session, put your work aside. Time will put distance between you and your words, allowing you to see them more clearly when you return to work on your poem again.

Don't be surprised if a poem takes longer than you planned. Creative work doesn't happen on a timetable. If you have to write a poem for class, make it as good as possible before you hand it in. Revise it later.

When you revise, be ruthless and gentle. Follow your instincts, and let the poem tell you how it wants to be.

Sometimes a poem will suggest its own shape: four lines the same length or a short line followed by a long line. If your poem suggests a form, re-write it that way.

Rhyme

If you've started a pattern of rhymes, follow it through. Rhyme creates expectation. In the poem "Alligator Pie," the first three lines

Alligator pie, alligator pie,
If I don't get some I think I'm gonna die.
Take away the green grass, take away the sky, . . .

lead you to expect the last line to rhyme, too. In fact, it does:

> *But don't take away my alligator pie.*

If it didn't, your ear would be disappointed. A poet might disappoint you on purpose, to focus your attention on the place where the pattern changed. But if there wasn't a good reason, you would be right to be annoyed.

Check to see that your rhymes make sense. Writers who have a good ear sometimes let the sound of the words drag them away from what they want to say. One student, for example, wrote in a serious poem about her pet:

> *I was as sad as sad could be.*
> *I saw my dog fly up a tree.*

Of course, her dog didn't fly. She was taken up with the sound of her words and lost track of what she wanted to say.

Perhaps you'll cut the rhymes altogether. If it's best for the poem, let them go.

Poetry should be true before it is beautiful. When you feel yourself being pulled toward a rhyme and away from the mysterious truth you are trying to express, resist rhyme. Tell the truth. And worry about how it sounds later.

Nouns and Verbs

Words are the basic units of a poem. Similes and metaphors are built of words. Words contribute their color and rhythm as well as their meaning to poems.

Nouns and verbs are the forceful, important words that give poems their spine.

Nouns name persons, places, things. *River* is a noun; so are *book, candle, door, face, shoe.* They are called common when they can describe any number of things. *Girl* can apply to any number of people and is a common noun. A proper noun, like *Mary,* is more specific.

It is important in poetry to be specific and precise. For example, if a poet writes, "My love is like

**Be specific. Why say "shell" if you can
say "conch," "scallop," "mussel," or "quahog"?**

a flower," that isn't as strong as writing "My love is like a red, red rose." A love like a red rose is easier to see and different from a love like a dandelion, a love like a tulip, or a love like a lilac.

Being specific helps your readers imagine exactly what you want to say. If you used a general noun—*flower, tree, animal, plant,* or *color*—tell your readers which one.

Verbs communicate energy and action. In "The Garden," Andrew Marvell wrote:

> *What wondrous life is this I lead!*
> *Ripe apples* **drop** *about my head;*
> *The luscious clusters of the vine*
> *Upon my mouth do* **crush** *their wine;*
> *The nectarine and curious peach*
> *Into my hands themselves do* **reach;**
> *Stumbling on melons, as I* **pass,**
> *Ensnared with flowers, I* **fall** *on grass.*

The verbs make the fruits seem almost alive!

Check your poem. Have you used forms of *to be—is, are, was, were*—or *to go—go, went, gone*—too often? Replace them with active verbs instead.

"We went into the ocean" is more colorful when rewritten as "We splashed into the waves."

Adjectives and Adverbs

Adjectives describe and modify nouns. Adverbs modify verbs. Both adverbs and adjectives are less useful in poems than nouns and verbs.

When you do use them, choose carefully. *Wondrous, ripe, curious*, and *luscious* are all adjectives. Perhaps the best is *curious*: it means both odd and nosy.

Beware of soft adjectives: *nice, pretty, good*. They don't tell the senses anything. What does *nice* look like? What does *pretty* feel like? What is the taste of something *good*? Be specific.

If you want to say your cat is pretty, tell us everything that makes her pretty: her color, size, the kind of fur she has, the way she walks, what sounds she makes, how she plays with you. It will make a more powerful poem.

Add details that appeal to the senses as you revise, too. Perhaps your cat is the color of butterscotch, or her purr sounds like a small motor running.

A Word of Encouragement

Writing poems takes patience. You can't hurry a flower into bloom or make a tree—or yourself—grow

49

Appeal to the senses. Call this cat "the color of butterscotch."

faster. And you can't rush a poem into completion. Work at it regularly, and your poem will be finished in its own good time.

Writing poems also takes practice. You learned to walk, to ride a bike, to read by practicing. You can learn to write poems that way, too.

CHAPTER FIVE

ENTERING THE WORLD OF POETRY

One of the best ways to learn more about poetry is by reading it. But with so much poetry out there, where do you begin?

Most students like the wise and witty work of **Shel Silverstein. Ogden Nash's** rhymes might make you laugh. The music and subjects of **Edgar Allan Poe** could appeal to you, too.

If you like tales of heroes, monsters, and adventures, read some epic poems in translation. The *Odyssey* and the *Iliad* by **Homer, Vergil's** *Aeneid,* and the Anglo-Saxon epic *Beowulf* are the source of many plots and characters that show up in superhero fantasy.

More modern American poets you might enjoy include **Robert Frost, Carl Sandburg, Walt Whit-**

Epic poems tell tales of wars and heroes. The Greek poet Homer wrote the story of the Trojan War in the *Iliad* and told of the adventures of the hero Odysseus (Ulysses) in the *Odyssey*.

Medusa, the snaky-haired monster of Greek mythology. Anyone who looked upon her directly was turned to stone, but the hero Perseus slew her by using his shield's shiny surface as a mirror.

man, William Carlos Williams, Emily Dickinson, and **Edna St. Vincent Millay.**

Gwendolyn Brooks and **Langston Hughes** are two black writers whose poetry is both accessible and important.

Some classic works that could please you include **Robert Louis Stevenson's** *A Child's Garden of Verses.* Or try the love poems of **Elizabeth Barrett Browning,** *Sonnets from the Portuguese.*

The work of **Frank O'Hara** appeals to many students. So do the shorter poems of **William Blake** and the poems of **Robert Burns,** such as "Ode to a Louse, Seen on a Lady's Hat in Church."

Anthologies of poetry are fun to read around in, too. *Talking to the Sun* includes poems from many centuries and around the world, along with wonderful artwork. *The Rattle Bag,* edited by Ted Hughes and Seamus Heaney, is excellent, too.

When you read an anthology and find a poet you like, look for a whole book of that poet's work. Spend some time with the poet, getting to know him or her better.

Ways to Learn More about Words

Whatever you're reading or writing, it helps to know more about words and the things they name.

Dictionaries are the place to look up the meaning and pronunciation of words that puzzle you. They can also help you learn more about the layers of meaning in a single word—its history, where it came from, where it was first used, all of the various meanings.

The thesaurus is another great source. Here you don't have to know what word you need, only what it means. You look up the meaning in a list in the back, and a number sends you to a section of the book where words that mean something like that are gathered. In some thesauruses, one side of the page holds one set of meanings; the other side lists opposites. Others are organized like dictionaries, with words in alphabetical order.

A caution: the thesaurus is full of fancy words that are very appealing. If you use lots of these words, you will write with a gaudy style. It's one way to do it.

But don't forget that simple language can move the heart and communicate mysteries and truth, too. And simple language makes it easier for the audience to understand. If you need a fancy word, fine. On the other hand, maybe you have a taste for fancy words. The American poet Wallace Stevens did. Experiment using big words and simple words, and see what you and your readers like best.

Field guides, dictionaries, and thesauruses
can help you learn the names of things. They are
useful both in reading and writing poems.

What's in a Name?

There are other ways to learn the names of things, and it's important to have words to name things precisely if you want to be a poet.

Why say "tree" when you could say ash or sassafras or spruce or maple or yew? To use these words well, you need to know what they signify. Nature guides are a way to learn the names of things in the world around us—weeds, birds, trees, wildflowers, animals, shells, different kinds of rock.

A new sort of book, the visual dictionary, supplies neatly labeled pictures showing what the parts of things are called. It's a great way to find the word for that thingamajig that goes between the doo-hickey and the whatziz on your bicycle.

Science books are another source of words and information. Botany, physics, chemistry—all of the sciences—will help you understand the world we live in, and that will help you write better poems.

Experts may be the best source. People who know about a particular thing are usually willing to help you learn the language of it. Beekeepers, cooks, and auto mechanics can teach you the language of their work and what they know about the world.

Experts can be rich sources of imagery that will help you learn ways to express yourself and your feelings more fully.

Learning about
Poetic Forms

Many reference books explain poetic form. Two good ones are *The Book of Forms* by Lewis Turco and *The Teachers & Writers Handbook of Poetic Forms*.

You may never want to write a ballad or a pantoum, but knowing they exist will help broaden your knowledge of poetry. And who knows, maybe the form of the villanelle or sonnet will appeal to you and enable you to say what is in your heart.

Publishing What You Write

If you want to publish what you write, you can send your work to a magazine, neatly typed, with your name and address in the upper left-hand corner and the poem centered on the page.

It's customary to include a stamped envelope, addressed to yourself, along with your poems. Some people include a short note, too.

How do you find a place to publish? Poets & Writers (72 Spring Street, New York, NY 10012) sells a list of magazines that publish the work of high school students. It includes places that publish work by younger people, too.

But the best way is to send your poems to magazines you read that publish poetry you like.

Publish Your Own Work

With personal computers and copying machines widely available, you can publish your own poems.

Type your poems or write them neatly. You can decorate your pages with artwork you do on the computer or draw by hand.

Then make copies. You can collect your poems in soft-cover binders or staple them together. A title and a nice cover for your collection will catch your reader's eye. Include just your own work or collect poems from friends.

Publishing your own poetry makes a good class project. And the finished collections make good gifts for parents and friends.

How to Get a Poet to Visit Your School

If you think it would be fun to have a poet come to your school, give you ideas for writing, and read what you wrote, you can probably make it happen.

Ask your teacher or your parents to request that a poet visit your class. Tell them that every state in the union has a poets-in-the-schools program. In most states, the state arts councils organize the program. Call or write the arts council to find out. Or the National Endowment for the Arts in Wash-

**Many poets visit schools to talk about
poetry and help students with their writing.
Why not invite a poet to your school?**

ington, D.C., can help you find poets-in-residence programs.

Poets who teach in schools bring in poems you'll enjoy reading. They will encourage you to write in class and to share your work. They can help make poetry real and live. You can learn from them: what they like and don't like can help you identify your strengths as a poet.

But if you can't get a poet to come to your school, don't despair. Poets are all around you, in every city and small town and in the countryside. They may be shy, though. In a world that measures success by the kind of car you drive, the job you hold, the size of the house you live in, some poets are like hermit crabs, living quietly, disguised as moms, dads, teachers, cabinetmakers, auto mechanics, or secretaries, and writing when they can.

Most love to talk about poetry, the way mothers and fathers love to talk about favorite children.

You will probably enjoy meeting some poets. May you also have the pleasure—at least for a little while—of being one, too.

FOR FURTHER READING

Heaney, Seamus, and Hughes, Ted, eds. *The Rattle Bag*. Faber and Faber, London, 1982. Poems arranged alphabetically by title. A splendid collection, worth finding.

Koch, Kenneth, and Farrell, Kate. *Talking to the Sun*. Henry Holt and Company, New York, 1985. A beautifully illustrated collection of poems from around the world.

Padgett, Ron, ed. *The Teachers & Writers Handbook of Poetic Forms*. Teachers & Writers Collaborative, New York, 1987. An excellent manual of forms, from abstract poems to word play.

Turco, Lewis. *The Book of Forms*. E. P. Dutton & Co., Inc., New York, 1968. A revised version, *The New Book of Forms*, appeared in 1986. The original is simpler and easier to use, with clear descriptions of everything from acrostics to villanelles.

INDEX

ACKNOWLEDGMENTS

P. 9: "Autobiographia Literaria" from COLLECTED POEMS OF FRANK O'HARA by Frank O'Hara. Copyright © 1967 by Maureen Granville-Smith, Administratrix of the Estate of Frank O'Hara. Reprinted by permission of Alfred A. Knopf, Inc.; p. 16: "Think of the storm roaming the sky uneasily . . ." from THE COMPLETE POEMS OF ELIZABETH BISHOP. Copyright © 1980 by Elizabeth Bishop. Reprinted by permission of Farrar, Straus & Giroux, Inc.; p. 19: "goodness was a fever in you" from BREATHING THE WATER by Denise Levertov. Copyright © 1987 by Denise Levertov. Reprinted by permission of New Directions Publishing Corporation; p. 21: "Miss Blues'es Child" from SELECTED POEMS by Langston Hughes. Copyright © 1959 by Langston Hughes. Reprinted by permission of Alfred A. Knopf, Inc.; "In Brueghel's great picture," p. 26: from THE COLLECTED POEMS OF WILLIAM CARLOS WILLIAMS, 1909–1939, vol. I., by William Carlos Williams. Copyright © 1938 by New Directions Publishing Corporation; p. 27: "Horses" by Robert Winner, courtesy of Sylvia Winner; p. 28: "André," from BRONZEVILLE BOYS AND GIRLS, by Gwendolyn Brooks. Copyright © 1956 by Gwendolyn Brooks. Reprinted by permission of HarperCollins Publishers; p. 42: "Alba" from PERSONAE by Ezra Pound. Copyright © 1926 by Ezra Pound. Reprinted by permission of New Directions Publishing Corporation; p. 45: "Alligator Pie" by Dennis Lee from *Alligator Pie*, published by Macmillan of Canada. Copyright © 1974 by Dennis Lee.

ABOUT THE AUTHOR

Margaret Ryan is a poet with two published books of poetry to her credit and has taught workshops for the Poets-in-Public-Service program in New York City. She holds a master's degree in poetry from Syracuse University and received the Davidson Award for sonnet writing from the Poetry Society of America in 1986. Ms. Ryan has also worked as a corporate speech writer, and her previous book for Franklin Watts was *So You Have to Give a Speech!* She lives in New York City with her husband and daughter.